Holiday
Activities

Rebecca Gilpin and Emily Bone

Designed and illustrated by
Non Figg, Molly Sage, Samantha Meredith
and Sharon Cooper

Edited by Phil Clarke

(Answers to puzzles are at the back.)

Which fish?

There are 37 fish on this page, but only 36 on the opposite page. Cross off the fish that are on both sides to find out which fish is missing.

Draw a line from the raft to the lake as fast as you can, without touching the banks of the river.

Draw some safari animals.

Draw lots of things on this island to make your own treasure map.

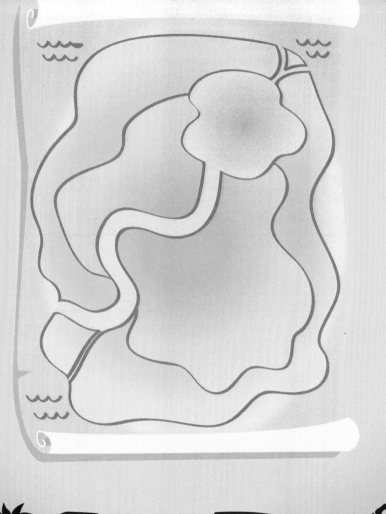

Decorate this mermaid's palace with
windows, doors and shells.

Stop the bus!

+ A game for two or more people

1. Everyone agrees on five categories, such as food, animals, countries, girls' names and boys' names, and writes them down.

2. One player thinks of a letter of the alphabet and says it out loud.

3. Everyone then tries to write something beginning with that letter in each of the categories. For the letter 'G' you could write grapes, gerbil, Greece, Grace and George.

4. The first person to write something for all five categories says "Stop the bus!" then everyone stops writing.

5. Everyone adds up their score. Each answer is worth two points, but if any players have the same answer, then they only get one point for it. The player who says "Stop the bus!" gets two bonus points.

6. Take it in turns to choose the letter. After six rounds, add up the final score. The winner is the person with the most points.

Draw the other half of this crab. Try to match it as closely as you can.

Draw more sharks in the sea.

Doodle shells and other things that could
have been washed up on the beach.

Beach jumble

Look at the jumbled shapes below and count
all the objects you might see on a beach.
Mark each one with a pen.

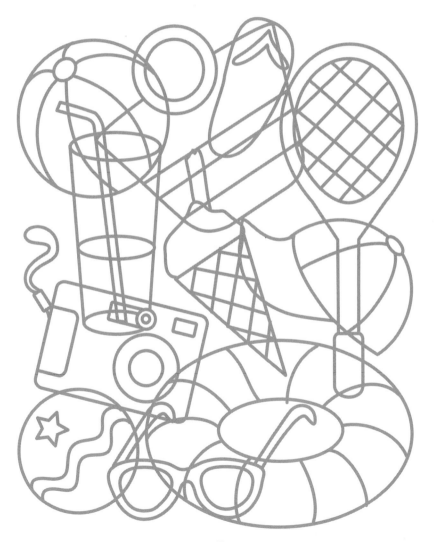

Doodle lots of things in this swimming pool.

Draw around each hoopla ring as quickly as you can without touching the prize.

Crab race

+ A game for two or more people

It's best to do this race on a sandy beach.

1. Draw lines in the sand to mark out a start line and a finish line about twenty steps away.

2. Each person gets on their hands and feet behind the start line, with their bodies sideways to the finish line.

3. Someone says "Ready, steady, GO!" and everyone scuttles sideways like crabs, until they reach the finish line. The winner is the first to cross the line.

Land, sea, air

+ A game for three or more people

1. Mark a line on the ground with a piece of chalk. Choose someone to be the commander. He stands at the end of the line and everyone else stands with one foot on either side of the line, facing him.

2. The commander shouts "land", "sea" or "air".

3. If the commander shouts "land" everyone jumps to the right of the line.

4. If the commander shouts "sea" then everyone jumps over to the left of the line.

5. For "air" everyone has to jump straight up in the air.

6. If "land" or "sea" are called twice in a row, everyone must stand still the second time. If they are called a third time, you jump again, and so on. If "air" is called two or three times in a row, everyone must jump twice the second time, three times the third time and so on.

7. Anyone who touches the line or makes a mistake is out of the game.

8. The last person still jumping is the winner and becomes the commander for the next game.

Decorate these sand castles.

20

Add lots of things to these pirate ships.

Sky jumble

Look at the jumbled shapes below and count
how many flying objects you can see.
Mark each one with a pen.

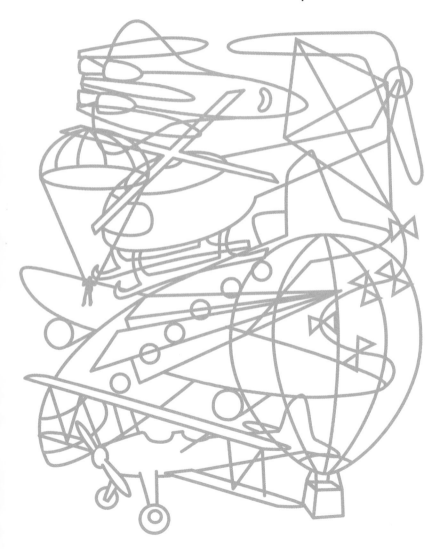

Draw what you might see on a tropical island.

French cricket

 + A game for three or more people

For this game you need a tennis ball and a cricket bat or tennis racket.

1. Choose someone to bat first. Everyone else spreads out all around him.

2. The batter stands holding the bat or racket down at his feet with his feet together, as shown in the picture. He is not allowed to move his feet from this position.

24

3. One of the other players bowls the ball at the batter, trying to hit him below the knees, while the batter tries to hit the ball.

4. If the batter hits the ball and no one manages to catch it, then he gets to keep on batting. Anyone can bowl the ball next.

5. The batter is out if someone catches the ball or if the ball hits him below the knees.

6. When a batter is out, he is replaced either by the person who bowled the ball (if it hit his legs) or by the person who caught it.

Draw a mouth, nose and sunglasses on the Sun.

Draw more monkeys in the trees.

Decorate these ice-cream cones.

Memory game

Look very carefully at this picture for
one minute then turn the page.

Memory game

Write down all the items you can remember from the other side of this page. There are 25 objects in total (things on a plate count as one object).

Bus tour

The bus is giving a tour of Santa Bona, visiting all the sights shown on the map below, before arriving at the hotel. The bus can't use the same stretch of road more than once. Draw the route the bus must use.

Hotel

What is it...?

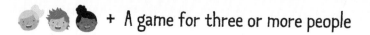

For this game, you need a pen or a pencil and some paper to draw on.

1. Choose one person to draw first. The other two players should sit on either side of her, so they can both see the paper easily.

2. The person drawing thinks of an object to draw, e.g. a boat. It shouldn't be anything that is too easy for the others to guess right away.

3. She starts to draw, and the other two players try to guess what she is drawing.

4. The first person to guess the picture correctly gets to draw next.

Another idea:

To make this game more difficult, the person drawing can draw the picture with their eyes closed. This makes it much harder for the others to guess what the picture is!

Add eyes, a nose, a mouth and some hair.

Draw faces on the roller coaster riders.

Sea change

There are ten differences
between these two pictures.

Circle each difference on this picture.

Down on one Knee!

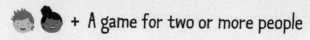

For this game of catch, you need a ball. Players should stand a little way away from each other. If there are more than two players, everyone should stand in a circle.

1. Take turns throwing the ball to each other.

2. If a player doesn't manage to catch the ball, the other players shout "Down on one knee!" and that player has to continue the game kneeling with one knee on the ground.

3. If that player drops the ball again, the others shout "One hand behind your back!" and he has to continue playing on one knee and with one hand behind his back, still trying to catch the ball.

4. The next time the same player drops the ball, everyone shouts "One eye closed!" and he has to close one eye.

5. If the same player drops the ball again, he is out of the game. The last person left in the game is the winner.

Draw a body, fins and a tail on this sea monster.

Doodle faces on the bus passengers.

Doodle patterns on the sails.

Picture pairs

All the pictures below have a matching picture somewhere on the next page. Look at this page for one minute and try to memorize the pictures and the numbers that go with them. Then, turn over and write the correct number on the matching pictures.

Picture pairs

Look at the instructions on the previous page.

Draw the view through the car windshield.

Jumbled jigsaw

The squares below have been taken from the picture.
Find where they have come from in the picture and
write down the correct number next to each square.

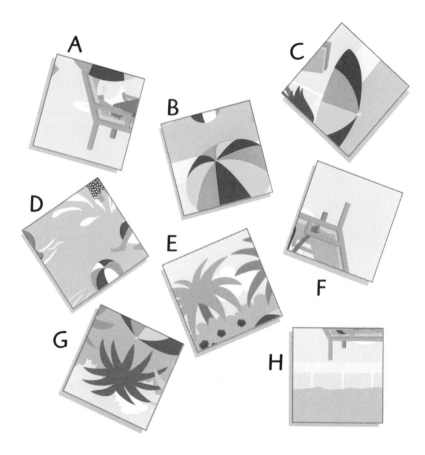

A

C

B

D

E

F

G

H

Who is it?

+ A game for three or more people

This game is best played inside, with any obstacles (e.g. chairs) moved out of the way.

1. One person is 'it' and stands in the middle of the room. 'It' wraps a scarf around her head so that she can't see.

2. Everyone else moves around the room. 'It' turns around three times, and then tries to 'tag' one of the other players.

um...

...is it Hannah?

3. When 'it' catches someone, she has to guess who they are by touching their face and hair.

4. If she doesn't guess correctly, she has to let the person go and the game continues.

5. When 'it' has caught someone and guessed who they are, that person becomes 'it' for the next game.

Draw a face on this mermaid and add
rows of scales on her tail.

Draw more fish.

Sardines

 + A game for four or more people

This game of hide-and-seek can be played inside or outside. If the game is played outside, then everyone should agree on the boundaries of the playing area before you start.

1. Choose one person to be the hider. Everyone else covers their eyes and counts to 50 while the hider finds a good place to hide.

2. As soon as the seekers have counted to 50, they spread out in all different directions to try to find the hider.

3. If one of the seekers finds the hider, they have to hide with them in the same place.

4. As each seeker finds the people hiding, they have to join them in the hiding place too.

5. The game continues until the last seeker finds all the other players hiding together.

Number letters

The aim of the game is to make words from the letters on the opposite page. Each letter is worth points. The player with the highest score wins.

1. For the first round, one player must choose one letter from each of the 'PLAYER 1' circles on the opposite page. Cross off each letter.

2. Player one then has one minute to make a word using these letters. You can use each letter once (although you don't have to use them all) and as many vowels as you like (but they don't score any points). You can also use '?' for any letter, but you will lose two points each time. Write the final word in the space below the circles.

3. The next player does the same using the 'PLAYER 2' circles. The letters don't have to be the same as the first player's letters.

4. Once each player has written a word, add up each score and write the scores in each 'Round 1' circle.

5. Play two more rounds, until all the letters have been crossed off.

6. Add up the total scores to find the winner.

A game for two people

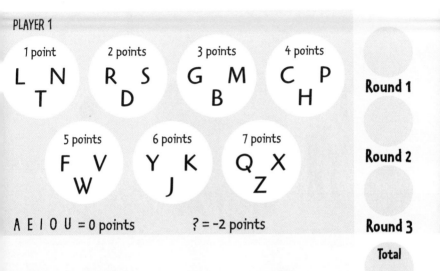

PLAYER 1

1 point	2 points	3 points	4 points
L N T	R S D	G M B	C P H

5 points	6 points	7 points
F V W	Y K J	Q X Z

A E I O U = 0 points   ? = -2 points

Round 1

Round 2

Round 3

Total

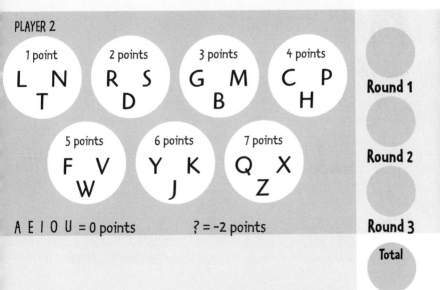

PLAYER 2

1 point	2 points	3 points	4 points
L N T	R S D	G M B	C P H

5 points	6 points	7 points
F V W	Y K J	Q X Z

A E I O U = 0 points   ? = -2 points

Round 1

Round 2

Round 3

Total

Word search

Find the animals hidden in the grid below and use the pen to draw a line through each word.

```
Y F X O F C I T C R A S
D J U E M P C K L A A N
R R C R L U O G R E L O
A E N M S A S C S W B W
P E W I L E T K O E A S
O D O N U I A Y O L T H
E N L E C G W L R X R O
L I F T I O N U N N O E
W E E B N R S E I I S H
O R E S O J G M P I S A
N O R A E B R A L O P R
S K I L L E R W H A L E
```

PENGUIN

ARCTIC TERN

WOLF

SNOW LEOPARD

MUSK OX

ALBATROSS

SNOWSHOE HARE

FUR SEAL

POLAR BEAR

KILLER WHALE

REINDEER

WALRUS

SNOWY OWL

ARCTIC FOX

ERMINE

Keep talking

1. Choose one person to be the referee. The other two people are the players.

2. The two players each choose a subject for the other person to talk about. This can be anything you like e.g. cars, food, films, aliens or even someone you both know. The subjects can be as silly as you like.

3. When the referee says "Go!" both players start talking about the subject that was picked for them.

I like pies. Fruit pies are the best
but I think if you put worms
in a pie I'd still eat it... um...

4. Both players have to keep talking for as long as they can, trying to ignore what the other person is saying.

5. You're not allowed to pause, say "um" or "er" or laugh. The referee listens carefully to make sure the players don't do any of these things.

6. When the referee hears someone break the rules, he declares the other person to be the winner. The referee's decision is final!

7. The loser becomes the referee in the next game, and the referee gets to play.

I think I am the BEST thing
in the whole world – so much better
than YOU...

Design your own flags.

Fill-in fun

Shade in all the shapes with dots inside
to discover what the picture is.

Codewords

On the right-hand page there is a grid
with a number in each square. Each
number stands for a letter of the
alphabet. You have to crack the code by
finding out all the words in the grid.
Three letters have already been decoded
to help you. Start by writing 'P' in all the
squares with number 6, then 'L' in all
the squares with number 18, and so on.

Read the instructions on the left-hand page, then fill in the grid below.

1	2	3	4	■	5	4	6	7	8	5	4	■
■	■	4	■	7	9	■	■	■	■	■	3	■
10	11	12	13	2	14	■	■	■	15	■	11	■
2	■	4	■	16	■	■	17	9	9	17	18	4
1	2	7	■	11	■	19	■	■	7	■	■	3
20	■	2	■	■	■	4	■	■	4	■	■	4
2	■	21	■	14	2	19	19	18	4	■	■	22
18	■	18	■	6	■	7	■	8	■	■	■	23
■	■	4	18	4	6	15	2	5	7	■	13	9
■	■	■	■	9	■	4	■	■	■	20	■	5
13	14	2	24	6	■	22	4	6	7	11	18	4
■	■	■	■	18	■	■	■	■	7	■	■	■
13	25	8	4	4	26	4	■	13	6	4	18	18

Fill in the letters below as you find them on the grid.

1	2	3	4	5	6	7	8	9	10	11	12	13
					P					I		
14	15	16	17	18	19	20	21	22	23	24	25	26
				L								

A	B	C	D	E	F	G	H	I	J	K	L	M
N	O	P	Q	R	S	T	U	V	W	X	Y	Z

63

Squiggle drawing

 + A game for two or more people

For this game you need some paper and two different pens or pencils.

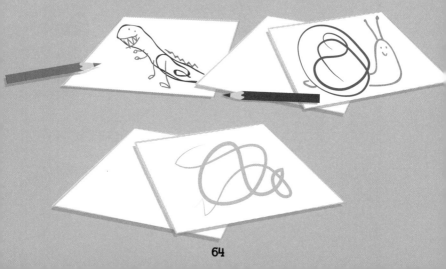

1. One person draws a squiggle on the paper.

2. The second person uses a different pen or pencil to turn the squiggle into a drawing. She can turn it into anything she likes, depending on the shape of the squiggle.

3. Take turns at drawing a squiggle, then turning it into a drawing. In the examples below, the same red squiggle has been turned into a puppy, a teapot and a girl with a ponytail. The only limit is your imagination!

Ground control

Can you find out which stand plane A is going to? Use the code on the right to help you follow the directions below and draw the correct route from the plane to its stopping point.

Move ahead

First right

First left

Stop!

Plane A

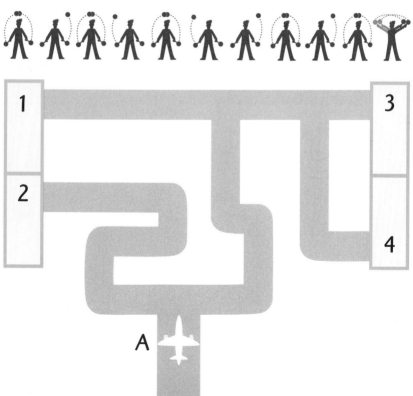

Look at the code on the left-hand page.
Use it to follow the directions below and
find out where each plane is stopping.

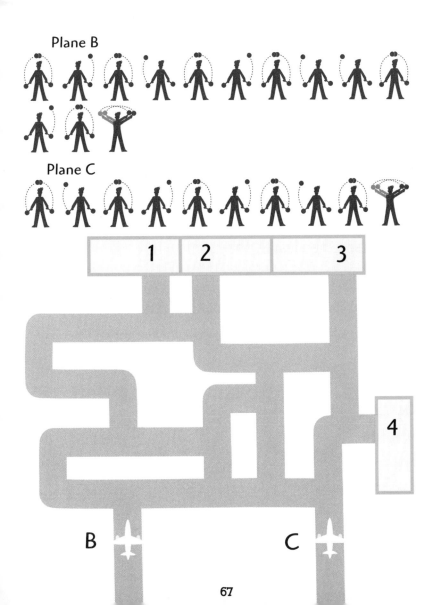

Plane B

Plane C

1   2   3

4

B   C

Monkey

 + A game for three or more people

This game is best played inside. The more players there are, the more fun it is to play.

1. Choose one person to be the guesser. The guesser then leaves the room.

2. While she is out of the room, everyone else decides who will be the 'monkey'. The other players will be the followers.

3. When the guesser comes back into the room, the monkey does an action, such as scratching his head or sticking out his tongue. The followers all copy whatever the monkey does.

4. The guesser has to determine which player is the monkey. The monkey does different actions for the followers to copy. He tries not to let the guesser see him changing the action.

5. When the guesser guesses who the monkey is, the monkey becomes the guesser for the next game.

Fill-in fun

Shade in all the shapes with dots inside to discover what the picture is.

Doodle monsters on these clouds.

Copycat

+ A game for two or more people

If there are two people playing this game, you should sit opposite each other. If there are more than two players, you should sit in a circle.

1. One person starts by doing an action, such as wiggling their nose.

2. The next person repeats the first action and then adds one of their own, such as clapping their hands together.

3. Everyone takes turns: each time repeating all the actions that have gone before, then adding a new action. The actions have to be repeated in the right order.

4. When someone forgets an action, or tries to do the actions in the wrong order, then they are out of the game. The winner is the last person left in the game.

Word games

Use the words in the orange circles to fill in the spaces below and make new words.

EAT

PIE

MOO

APE

SIT

COD

LAY

USE

LID

MAN

1. S __ __ __ TH

2. VI __ __ __ OR

3. M __ __ __ UM

4. SW __ __ __ ER

5. MA __ __ __ SIA

6. CO __ __ __ D

7. SH __ __ __ S

8. HO __ __ __ AYS

9. GER __ __ __ Y

10. CRO __ __ __ ILE

Each pair of words below can be linked by another
word to make two new words or phrases.
For example: DAISY C H A I N MAIL to make
'daisy chain' and 'chain mail'.
Fill in the linking words in the pairs below.

1. CARD __ __ __ __ __ GAME

2. HONEY __ __ __ STING

3. RAIN __ __ __ TIE

4. TEA __ __ __ CAKE

5. BALLPOINT __ __ __ FRIEND

6. SWIM __ __ __ __ CASE

7. BEACH __ __ __ __ GOWN

8. FRYING __ __ __ CAKE

9. NEWS __ __ __ __ __ CHAIN

10. AIR __ __ __ __ HOLE

In my backpack...

 + A game for two or more people

1. Someone begins the game by saying "In my backpack, I have..." followed by an object. For example, you could start with "In my backpack, I have a soggy sandwich."

2. Someone else repeats what the first person has said, then adds another object. It makes the game funnier if the objects are not related to each other in any way, such as: "In my backpack, I have a soggy sandwich and a rusty trumpet."

3. Everyone takes it in turns to add items to the backpack, each time repeating the growing list of items that are already in there. The items must be repeated in the correct order.

4. When someone forgets an item, or tries to say the list in the wrong order, then that person is out of the game. The winner is the last player left in the game.

Brain benders

The chairs by Bluesea Beach are so big that you can't see how many people are sitting there from behind. See if you can determine the smallest number of chairs that could be occupied if all the following information is true:

1. A boy is sitting to the right of a girl

2. A girl is sitting to the right of a girl.

3. Two girls are sitting to the left of a boy.

There are nine bottles and four large beach bags.
Without leaving any out, how can you put an
odd number of bottles into each bag?
(Clue: each bag can hold up to nine bottles.)

Add more penguins.

Turn these fingerprints into fish, shells or crabs.

Hotter or colder?

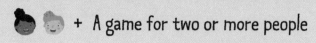 + A game for two or more people

This game is best played inside. You'll need a small object like a pencil or a coin, or something else that can be easily hidden.

1. Choose one person to be the seeker. She must leave the room.

2. One of the other players hides the object somewhere in the room.

FREEZING COLD!

3. When the object has been hidden, the players call the seeker back into the room. The seeker moves slowly around the room, trying to find the object.

4. As she moves away from the object, everyone shouts "Colder!", "Very cold!" or even "Freezing cold!" As she gets closer to the object, everyone shouts "Warmer!", "Hotter!" or even "Boiling hot!" The seeker follows these directions until she finds the object.

5. Take turns to be seeker.

BOILING HOT!

Doodle a big sunhat on this dog.

Starting at the arrow, draw the tower without going over the same line twice.

Cross code

Read the next page to find out what to do.

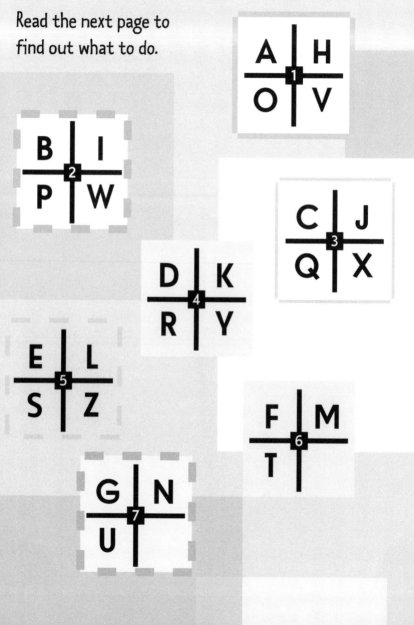

For this code, use the crosses on the opposite page. To start with, find the letter you want to put into code. For example, if you wanted to put the letter 'D' into cross code, you would find it on cross no. 4:

Write ⌐ to show where the letter appears on the cross, and 4 to show which cross the letter appears in, like this: 4⌐

Try writing your name in cross code:

Use the cross code to decode these messages:

1. ⌐1 1⌐ ⌐7 5⌐   ⌐4 7⌐ 7⌐   2⌐ 1⌐ 3⌐4 5⌐ 4⌐

⌐4 7⌐ 7 4⌐   6⌐ 7⌐ 7 6⌐1 2⌐ 4⌐ 7⌐ 5⌐1

2. 2⌐ 7⌐ 7⌐   7 7⌐⌐4 1⌐ 7 5⌐

Where in the world?

 + A game for two or more people

1. Someone begins the game by saying the name of a place. It can be the name of a town, a city or a country, e.g. Sweden.

2. The next person has to say a place name beginning with the last letter of that place. In this case, it would be a place beginning with 'N' e.g. New York.

New York

3. The game continues with players taking turns to say a place name. In this example, the next player might say Kenya, or Kuala Lumpur.

4. If someone can't think of a place, they are out of the game.

5. The winner is the last person left in the game.

Kenya

Write or doodle in the travel diary.

Today I went to...

...and saw...

Decorate the hot-air balloons.

Story consequences

+ A game for two or more people

1. Everyone writes a word that can describe a man, such as 'happy', at the top of a strip of paper. Fold back the top of the paper to hide the word, then pass it to the next player.

2. Each person writes a man's name (it can be someone famous, or someone you all know) before folding the paper and passing it on.

3. Add the following things one at a time: a word to describe a woman, a woman's name, a place, what the man says to the woman, what she says to him and what happens at the end.

4. Everyone unfolds the paper they are holding. Each person then makes a story out of the words on the strip, like this:

'Happy Dr. Dolittle met pretty Cinderella at the Eiffel Tower. He said to her "These cakes are good." She said to him "I prefer cats." Then a cow fell out of the sky.'

Design some stamps.

Drawing lines

Draw over all the lines in each shape below
without going along any of the lines twice,
or taking your pen off the page.

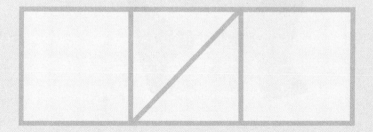

Picture consequences

 + A game for two or more people

1. The game starts with each person drawing a head and neck at the top of a long strip of paper. They then fold the paper back so that the head is hidden, but the bottom of the neck can still be seen.

2. Each paper is passed to someone else, who then draws a body and arms, as far as the waist, and folds the paper over.

3. The papers are passed on again, and everyone draws legs, as far as the ankles. The papers are folded and passed on again.

4. Each person adds feet to their picture, before the papers are folded again and passed on.

5. Everyone unfolds the piece of paper that they have, to see the silly picture on it.

Stars and stripes

For this puzzle, add stars to the grid below, following the rules about where stars can and can't be placed:

1. Every striped square must have one star next to it, either horizontally or vertically.

2. Stars cannot be placed next to each other horizontally, vertically or diagonally.

3. The numbers next to the grid show how many stars must be in that row or column.

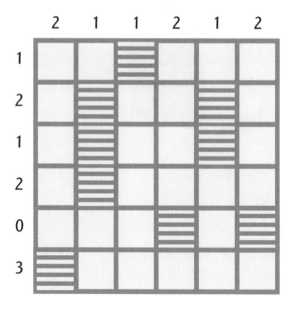

Design a cover for a travel guide.

Egypt

Gold Coast

Fun World

Holland

Draw a treehouse in the tree.

Draw a line to show which way the campers should go to reach their tent.

Guess the song

+ A game for two or more people

1. One person thinks of a song for the others to try to guess.

2. They then hum the first line of the song and the others try to guess what it is. Each person has one guess. If someone gets it right, it is their turn to think of a song.

3. If no one guesses correctly, the first person then hums the first and second lines, and everyone has another guess.

4. The game continues with the person who is humming adding one line at a time, and the others trying to guess what the tune is.

5. If no one has guessed after one whole verse, the person who is humming says what the song is. They then have another turn.

Turn these shapes into cars, trucks and buses.

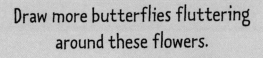

Draw more butterflies fluttering
around these flowers.

Feed the shark

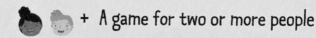 + A game for two or more people

This game is best played on a sandy beach.

1. Copy the shape on the next page to trace out a shark's head in the sand – use your finger or a stick. The shark's head can be made bigger to make the game easier, or smaller to make it harder.

2. Draw a line in the sand about five big steps away from the shark. Everyone stands behind this line to play.

3. Take turns trying to throw a pebble or a shell into the shark's mouth. If you manage to do this, you get two points. If your pebble lands on the shark (but not in the mouth) you get one point. You don't get any points if it lands anywhere else!

4. The first person to reach ten points wins.

Line-up

+ A game for two people

The object of the game is to line up four of the same symbols in a vertical, horizontal, or diagonal line. Before you start, decide who will be 'O' and who will be 'X', and who will take first turn.

1. The first player chooses a column, then draws their symbol in a square on the bottom row, like this. The next player chooses another column and draws their symbol in the square on the bottom row.

O X

2. Players take turns drawing their symbols in the grid. A player must draw his symbol in the lowest blank square of any column.

X
O X O
O X X X O

3. The winner is the first person to line up four symbols.

O
X O X
O X O
O X X X O

Draw kites on the end of the lines.

Puzzle answers

2. Which fish?

This is the missing fish

13. Beach jumble

Beach ball, glass with straw, sandal, racket, baseball cap, inflatable ring, ice cream cone, sunglasses, small ball, beach bag, camera.

22. Sky jumble

Rocket, parachute, helicopter, boomerang, hot-air balloon, plane, bi-plane, kite, paper plane.

31. Bus tour

36. Sea change

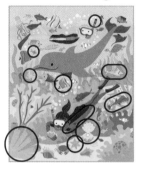

46. Jumbled jigsaw

A:34 B:29 C:26 D:24 E:9 F:31
G:7 H:16

57. Word search

61. Fill-in fun

62. Codewords

1 C	2 A	3 V	4 E	5 N	6 P	7 T	8 U	9 O	10 J	11 I	12 G	13 S
14 W	15 H	16 X	17 D	18 L	19 F	20 K	21 B	22 R	23 Y	24 M	25 Q	26 Z

66. Ground control

Plane A goes to stand 3
Plane B goes to stand 2
Plane C goes to stand 3

70. Fill-in fun

74. Word games

1. SMOOTH 2. VISITOR
3. MUSEUM 4. SWEATER
5. MALAYSIA 6. COPIED
7. SHAPES 8. HOLIDAYS
9. GERMANY 10. CROCODILE

1. BOARD 2. BEE 3. BOW
4. CUP 5. PEN 6. SUIT 7. BALL
8. PAN 9. PAPER 10. PORT

78. Brain benders

The smallest number of people sitting in the deck chairs is three.

Put three bottles into three of the bags. Then, put all the bags into one bag.

86. Cross code

1. Have you packed your toothbrush? 2. Bon voyage!

95. Drawing lines

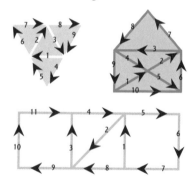

98. Stars and stripes

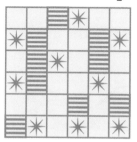